A special gift from


To


D0709598

**Other Helen Exley Giftbooks**
Woof!                          365 Days with my faithful Dog
Utterly Adorable Cats          365 Days with my bossy Cat
Utterly Lovable Dogs

Published in 2012 by Helen Exley Giftbooks in Great Britain.

**Edited by Dalton Exley**
Photography copyright © Yoneo Morita 2012 Hanadeka™
Licensed through Intercontinental Licensing
**Words by Pam Brown** © Helen Exley Creative Ltd 2012
Design, selection and arrangement © Helen Exley
Creative Ltd 2012

12 11 10 9 8 7 6 5 4 3 2 1

**ISBN: 978-1-84634-679-8**

**Helen Exley Giftbooks**
16 Chalk hill, Watford, Herts,
WD19 4BG, UK.

To view the complete list of Helen Exley gifts,
please visit our website:
**www.helenexleygifts.com**

Follow us on  and

A PURRFECT GIFTBOOK

# Meow!

BY PAM BROWN

Photographs by Yoneo Morita
Edited by Dalton Exley

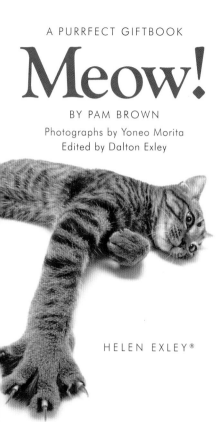

HELEN EXLEY®

A cat
brings beauty into
the dullest day.

A small cat
in the window,
a small cat
at the door.
And there is love.

A little cat brings
the jungle
into suburbia.

Every tamed
cat is a small,
amiable tyrant.

A sleeping cat
has discovered
the secret of
perfect content.

All cats have
a surprise up
their sleeves.

All cats are beautiful even the ugly ones.

A dog looks guilty if he's sinned. A cat, never.

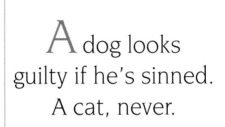

A dog serves.
A cat is served.
Preferably
with haddock.

Cats never lose
the chance to steal
a scene.

A cat can always manage a second breakfast – donated by the kind lady up the road. Or a third. Or a fourth.

Anyone who has
a cat suspects that
it is psychic.

A kitten is only
a beginning –
a prelude to
the glory of cathood.

A reformed
street cat can be
the sweetest natured
of them all.

Cats never
perform to order.

ANOTHER WORD FOR
FASTIDIOUS IS CAT.

Cats know, quietly and with complete conviction, that they are the superior species.

Cat. Remember me.
Come home.

A dog secretly hopes that one day he will become human. A cat would be appalled by the possibility.

Every movement
a cat makes has
been perfected
through millennia.
And he knows it.

A dog loves
to be laughed at.
A cat takes
a long while
to forgive you.

Cats are not
Almost Human.
They are
totally Cat.

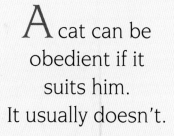

A cat can be
obedient if it
suits him.
It usually doesn't.

A cat can beg,
implore, beseech
without twitching
a whisker.

Every cat,
pampered or
scruffy, stray
or sheltered
is utterly unique
and worthy
of respect.

$A$ little cat
has taught many a child
to care, to love.

"As helpless
as a kitten."
is a nonsense.
Kittens cope.

A cat cannot
speak but she can
still give orders.

A dog performs
to delight his owner,
a cat to delight
himself.

A very small
cat can dominate
a household.

Any competent psychiatrist confronted with analysis of a feline mind would be driven to retirement after a single session.

Be alert. Your cat can out-think you.

"Ah," say
the dog owners
"He's nearly human."
Cat owners
would not dare.

A little cat, a little lonely cat. Hurt. Afraid. Astounded by kindness. Rescued. Safe.
A little cat. A little life.
A little hope for humankind.

Buy in bulk
the food your cat
adores – and be
withered with contempt
"That...?"

Cats know all about cameras. And which is their Best Side.

A kitten believes
all things are
permissible
so long as they
are fun.

Call a dog
and he comes.
Call a cat and
he may.
Eventually.

Every tiny bundle
of fur is fully armed.

Every cat a tiger
in disguise.

All over the world people are sitting, or lying, in extreme discomfort rather than disturb the cat.

All cats – from Bengal Tigers to alley cats – are variations on a single splendid theme.

Fire, flood
or earthquake.
What one treasure
would I choose to save?
You, of course,
dear cat.

A mind. A heart.
A little loving,
living cat as my
companion.

Cats are mysterious,
elegant, beautiful.
Cats are ridiculous,
unpredictable, manipulative,
stubborn, dictatorial, picky.
Cats are dim-witted. Ingenious
Inventive. Cats get under foot,
take over chairs and beds, sulk
Are deeply disobedient.
Love as they choose to love.
Cats are who they decide to be
One is never, never dull with a
cat as companion.

And yet, dear cat, exasperating cat, we love you. We turn to you in sadness, in loneliness, in sickness. Dear cat. Dear comfort. Dear friend.